I dedicate this book to my family, with special thanks
to my mother Janet. I love you all.

In addition, I'd like to thank all those who believed in me,
and especially those who did not.

–1–

A drop of sweat fell in my eye
and I missed the ball.

–2–

I stubbed my toe on the base of my bed,
now I can't wear my golf shoes.

–3–

I've only played with these clubs twice.

–4–

My rain suit is too tight and
I can't swing my club smoothly.

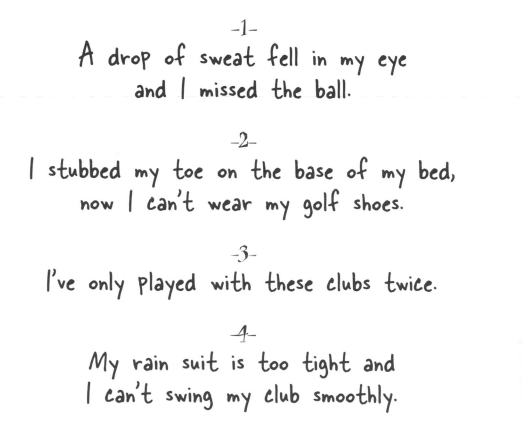

= 1

-5-

My ball is all scuffed up.

-6-

I keep picking up my head. I'm afraid the geese are going to do their business on me.

-7-

The tee was leaning too far forward.

-8-

I get nervous hitting last all the time.

–9–
The sun was in my eyes.

–10–
I have tendonitis in my left foot.

–11–
My dog chewed up my golf glove.

–12–
I just took a lesson and I can't
get used to my new setup and grip.

-13-

I hit it off the heel of the club.

-14-

My clubs need to be regripped.
They keep slipping out of my hand.

-15-

I'm missing some spikes on my
golf shoes and it makes me slip.

-16-

I thought you said, "Dog leg left."

-17-

I thought this was the nine iron, not the six.

-18-

It's this new putter.

-19-

The greens are a lot faster than they look.

-20-

These new shoes are killing me.
I think I'll get a cart for the back nine.

-21-

The golfers on the other tee box were talking and I couldn't concentrate.

-22-

The ball washer was out of water. I couldn't focus with that speck of dirt on the ball.

-23-

Did you see that? A bug landed on my ball just as I was starting my downswing!

-24-

The wind was with me when I was lining up the shot.

6

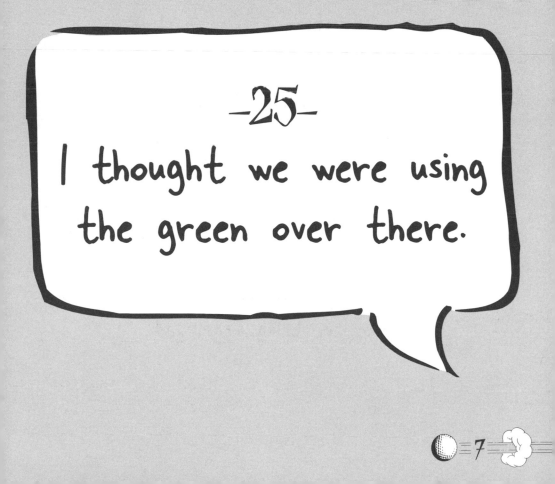

-26-
It's my first time out this year.

-27-
This is my first time out
since my bypass operation.

-28-
I left my sunglasses in my other golf bag.

-29-
These are my wife's clubs.
Mine are being regripped.

-30-

It must have kicked the wrong way off the hill, because the shot looked perfect.

-31-

I didn't follow through on the swing.

-32-

It's just too hot to be playing golf.

-33-

It's just too cold to be playing golf.

-34-

My ball isn't white.
I can only play with white golf balls.

-35-

This ball is white.
I only play well when I use pink golf balls.

-36-

I've run out of white tees.
I only play well with white tees.

-37-

My caddie gave me the wrong club.

-38-
My knee hurts from an old
high school football injury.

-39-
I didn't follow through with my hips.

-40-
I'm doing exactly what my golf instructor
told me to do, but the ball keeps slicing.

-41-
A pebble deflected my putt to the left.

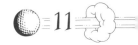
=11=

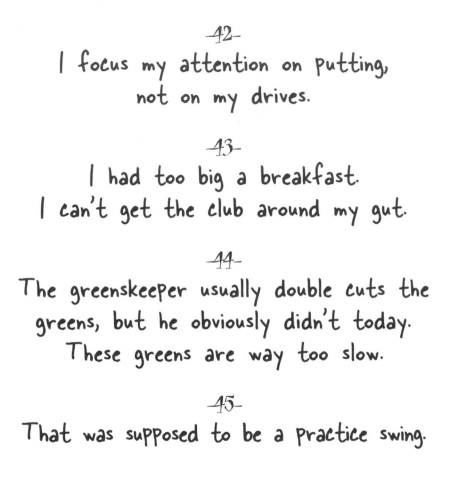

-42-

I focus my attention on putting,
not on my drives.

-43-

I had too big a breakfast.
I can't get the club around my gut.

-44-

The greenskeeper usually double cuts the
greens, but he obviously didn't today.
These greens are way too slow.

-45-

That was supposed to be a practice swing.

-46-

I can't remember if I'm supposed to inhale or exhale at impact.

47-

I just didn't get all of the ball.

-48-

My dog urinated on my good golf shoes so I have to play in my sneakers.

-49-

There's a nick on my ball, so it spun out of bounds.

–51–

These are new clubs.

–52–

I took too much of the earth on that swing.

–53–

There's too much sand in these bunkers.

–54–

Boy, the greenskeeper must be in an awful mood. I've never seen so many tough pin positions.

–55–

I didn't have time to warm up.
I usually hit a bucket of balls before playing.

–56–

The airline lost my clubs—again.
I'm having to use rentals.

–57–

Those hedges were just planted.
That's a do-over.

–58–

My socks are wet from the rain.
I keep slipping in my shoes.

The group ahead of us is playing too slow.
It's throwing off my rhythm.

I can't play on this course.
I haven't been able to
practice it on virtual golf.

It's impossible to get a true roll on these
greens—no one repairs their ball marks here.

I hit it off the toe of the club.

-63-
I left my lucky visor in the car.

-64-
I didn't have lunch.
I have no energy.

-65-
This course does not have the
yardage marked accurately.
There is no way that was 139 yards.

-66-
I must be allergic to the pesticide spray.
My eyes keep watering and I can't see the ball.

-67-

Taking a cart throws my timing off.
I usually visualize my next shot as
I am walking up to the ball.

-68-

It must have been that last beer.
I had a great round going.

-69-

I couldn't see from back there that it
was not a vertical water hazard.

-70-

I quit smoking yesterday.

-71-
Since canceling my subscription to Golf Digest,
I just don't play well.

-72-
The putting green was closed this morning.

-73-
I was thrown out of my
Tuesday evening group for slow play,
so I haven't been able to get out regularly.

-74-
I lost one of my contacts and
the flagstick is all fuzzy.

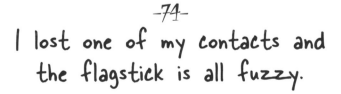

75

If the pin was pulled, it would have gone in.

-76-
I didn't know it was against the rules to tell a competitor what club I used.

-77-
I thought you get a mulligan every hole. That's the way I was taught.

-78-
My golf glove is wet. I can't get a grip on the club.

79-
I've been working on my MBA. I just haven't had time to practice.

-80-
The slope on that green is subtle but severe.

-81-
The ground is too dry.
My divots aren't coming off smoothly.

-82-
My neck is stiff;
I must have slept on it wrong.

-83-
The driving range uses a
different type of golf ball.
I can't seem to gauge my distance.

23

-84-

I'm too busy at work to get away and play.
I'm inconsistent.

-85-

My wife won't let me
play since having the kid.
I knew I should have gotten a dog instead.

-86-

The driving range was closed.

-87-

I'm having trouble adjusting to these
left-handed clubs—but I did save $20.

-88-

My back is sunburned.
It hurts to swing.

-89-

I'm still depressed from the
18 holes yesterday.

-90-

The nearest golf course is
200 miles from my house.

-91-

My rain suit is at home.
I don't play well while wearing wet clothes.

-92-
My wife is pregnant and
I can't get any sleep.

-93-
I have tennis elbow.
What the heck is tennis elbow anyway?

-94-
That acorn threw off my putt.

-95-
I've had to play softball every
Saturday and Sunday this summer.
I just haven't been out.

-96-

I haven't had any money to play;
my school loans are due.

-97-

I always get kicked off the course
for being intoxicated.
This is the first round
I've finished in over two years.

-98-

The sunscreen I put on my hands
made them greasy and my club slipped.

-99-

I have a tear in my golf glove.

 = 27

–100–

I don't know why
I bought clubs
with graphite shafts.
Steel is the way
to go.

28

-101-

This course doesn't let you chip
on the practice green.

-102-

My short game is not what
I focused on in my last lesson.

-103-

I forgot to take my watch off and
it threw off my balance.

-104-

My putting lesson was rained out last week.

-105-

I ran out of tees, so I had to use half a tee and I couldn't get the loft required to fly the trap.

-106-

I cut my hand at work, so I can't get a firm grip on the clubs.

-107-

I have a headache from the concert last night. I just can't concentrate.

-108-

It rained all week and I couldn't practice.

I thought this was a par–5, not a 4!
I was laying up on my second shot.

It was a tough week at work and I don't seem
to have any energy left for my golf game.

I'm getting tired.
I usually take a cart.

Did you see that? That bird deflected
my shot into the woods!

–113–

I have to accept that my swing speed
is decreasing now that I'm over 50.

–114–

You should have told me about
the water on this hole.

–115–

This is one of those courses you need to play a
few times before you can expect to score well.

–116–

I don't have a sand wedge.
I lost it in the lake last time I played.

-117-
I didn't open my stance and
I pushed the ball to the left.

-118-
My shoes aren't tied tightly enough.

-119-
Someone stole my good clubs because
I forgot to set the alarm on my golf bag.

-120-
I forgot my antacid and I have bad
indigestion from eating so many Milk Duds
while watching Caddyshack last night.

33

-121-

Those guys were making too much
noise on the other fairway.

-122-

I usually play from the championship tees.
Moving up confuses me.

-123-

I can't play my best when
I have to wait between shots.
What's taking those guys so long?

-124-

The greens are much faster in Florida.

-125-

This area wasn't considered out of bounds last year.

-126-

I pushed my hips too much while trying
to get out of that fairway trap.

-127-

The ball should go left if
the ball is above my feet.

-128-

I can't keep my head still on the backswing.

-129-

I moved my body too far forward on
impact and sliced it into the fairway,
but it rolled into the woods.

-130-

I have a bad case of jet lag.

-131-

My other driver has a 11.5-degree loft.
I can't hit a 9-degree driver.

-132-

I didn't keep my left arm in.
I hate this game.

-133-

I gripped the club too far
down and topped the ball.

-134-

I just can't keep my mind off of her;
it's so frustrating.
Where is the beer girl anyway?

-135-

I don't know what the hell is wrong.

-136-

These greens have way too much sand on them.
It slows down all my putts.

-137-

Do those ducks ever quit quacking?
I can't believe how loud they are.

-138-

I didn't have oatmeal for breakfast—I only
play well when I eat oatmeal for breakfast.

-139-

The ranger keeps following me around.
I can't focus when I'm being watched.

-140-

I ate way too much on the turn;
now I'm bloated.

-141-

The hail keeps hitting my eyes.
Maybe we should wait until the storm passes.

-142-

The balls fly much farther in Colorado.
I can't get my distance gauged.

-143-

My wrists aren't breaking on impact.

-144-

I have a bad back from
rugby practice yesterday.

-145-

Those low-flying airplanes are really annoying.

-146-
That bee must be addicted to my cologne.
It keeps following me from hole to hole.

-147-
The fairway looks like it slopes to the left,
not the right.

-148-
My hands were too far
to the left on my grip.

-149-
I keep closing the club face and
I can't get the loft to clear the red tees.

-150-

I can't get loose—
my chiropractor is
out of town.

42

-151-

I pulled a muscle in my leg while helping an elderly lady get her bag out of the car trunk.

-152-

I've lost all my money gambling and now I can't afford lessons.

-153-

My wife was awarded my twenty-two backup putters in the divorce settlement, and now I have to play with this darn thing.

-154-

My grip just isn't comfortable.

-155-

I hurt my hips having sex last night.

-156-

The sand trap should not be right
in the middle of the fairway.
Oh, I thought that was our fairway.

-157-

I slept on my shoulder the wrong way.
Now my swing is all messed up.

-158-

I wanted to practice, but the
range was out of balls.

44

-159-
I focus too much on where the ball is going.
I can never follow through.

-160-
Those swing machines are too expensive.

-161-
Damn it, have you no etiquette?
Please quit breathing when I swing.

162-
The instructor told me to play my
slice and now I hit the ball straight.

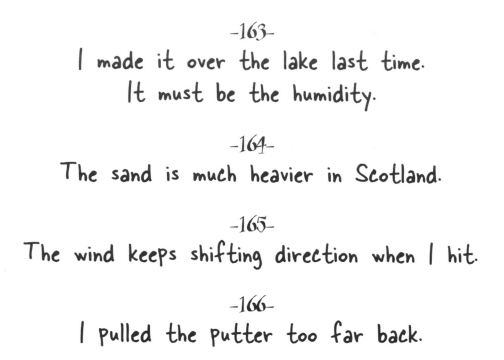

-163-
I made it over the lake last time.
It must be the humidity.

-164-
The sand is much heavier in Scotland.

-165-
The wind keeps shifting direction when I hit.

-166-
I pulled the putter too far back.

-167-
I duffed the shot.
No excuse for that.

-168-
I'm just not releasing on the ball.

-169-
I hurt my elbow when
I got out of that damn cart.

-170-
My old caddy's notes are in Japanese and I
can't interpret them since he was deported.

-171-

I lined up with the ball too
close to my left foot.

-172-

These balls don't fly as far as yours,
but I got a good deal on mine.

-173-

When I'm on the practice tee
the ball always goes straight.

-174-

Didn't you hear that sound in the woods
during my swing? It sounded like a duck.

-175-

My swing looks perfect on video; I don't know what's wrong.

-176-

I just need to work on my grip.

-177-

I just don't have any rhythm today.
I need to listen to some music.

-178-

I forgot about that trap
in front of the green.

-179-

I am hitting the ball too perfectly.
It keeps going too far.

-180-
I keep pulling the ball.
It must be the aerobics I've been taking.

-181-
Damn it! Damn it! Damn it!

-182-
I needed to use a seven, not an eight,
just short of a hole in one.

-183-
I'm getting off the tee fine—
it's my short game that is so bad.

–184–

When I yelled "fore," my caddie
thought that was the club I needed.

–185–

I play better with women.
They motivate me.

–186–

I decided to become celibate yesterday.

–187–

Someone left a cigar burning on the
green and it made my putt drift.

-188-
I hate these soft spikes.
I keep slipping.

-189-
I played the ball too far back in my stance
and I couldn't get it over that tree.

190-
I always have trouble focusing on the
ball when the sun is setting.

-191-
These balatas spin too much.
I like a harder—shelled ball.

-192-

My backswing is way too short.

-193-

I was up all night watching M*A*S*H reruns.
I didn't get any rest.

-194-

I took too much sand on that swing.

-195-

I never follow through when
trying to get out of a bunker.

-196-

I always choke when money is on the line.

-197-

I always aim too far left
when coming out of the bunker.

198-

My arm moved too far
to the left of the vertex.

-199-

Rough should test you,
not penalize you one stroke.
This is unfair.

-201-

That Golf Channel has me all screwed up.

-202-

I never had a shot—the tree was in the way.

-203-

Fore!!!!!!!!!

-204-

Ever since I made a hole in one,
I can't concentrate.

–205–

I read way too much into the putts.

–206–

My backswing is too flat.

–207–

The wind is chasing us.
It seems like we are always
playing into the wind.

–208–

I just can't gauge the chipshots like I used to.

–209–

I can't get my wedge to bite.

–210–

My ball was buried in the
middle of a footprint.
Some idiot didn't rake the trap.

–211–

I've been going at the
flagstick way too often.

–212–

The practice green was much faster.

-213-

I need to relax and take a deep breath.
I'm playing way too fast.

-214-

I forgot my umbrella in the car.
Now my glasses are foggy.

-215-

I never saw the break from that angle.

-216-

I lifted the tip of the putter
too high off the ground.

-217-

I have to go to the bathroom;
I can't concentrate.

-218-

It's only the 18th hole.
I'm not quite warmed up yet.

-219-

I never tilted my shoulders.

-220-

My angle of impact exceeded the reflection
angle, causing me to duff the shot.

-221-

When the hole was moved, the greenskeeper
left a gap in the green.
There goes my eagle.

-222-

So what if it was a three-footer? I was
only trying to get the ball close, not make it.

-223-

I knew I had a mulligan left!

-224-

The weatherman said it was going to warm up.
I should have brought my sweater, I'm chilly.

–225–

It's not my swing—
it's these old clubs!

-226-

I just can't generate the power
that I could when I was young.

-227-

I'm sorry I'm playing so poorly.
My wife reminded me that I'm scheduled
for my annual checkup tomorrow.

-228-

My boss is a jerk.
I can't relax.

-229-

All the golf schools I liked were too expensive—
so I'm self-taught.

-230-

I had a blind shot, but the ball went where I hit it. I just didn't see the pond.

-231-

I usually walk.
This "riding in a cart" is not allowing me to find my rhythm.

-232-

I just want the most strokes for the money—to heck with my score.

-233-

My dog chewed a hole in my good golf shoes.

-234-

I can't play in 70-degree, sunny weather.
I need snow, wind, and rain.

-235-

All the weightlifting I'm doing has
made me too huge for golf.

-236-

My pager vibrated during that putt.

-237-

Tournament pressure is hard to handle.

-238-
The slow play throws off my concentration.
It shouldn't take 5-1/2 hours for a round.

-239-
I only play well on hilly courses.

-240-
You should have seen me play last week.

-241-
I left my new clubs in my other car.

-242-

The geese keep following me.
It makes me nervous.

-243-

I had to lay up; I was just using the
3-wood for the heck of it.

-244-

My usual golf cart is electric.
This gas-powered one is
uncomfortable and noisy.

-245-

I never aligned the club face on my setup.

68

-246-

I usually use titanium clubs.
These tungsten clubs are too light.

-247-

My other driver is a 8.5-degree loft,
not a 10-degree. I'm losing too much
distance out of the box.

-248-

My children don't count my whiff.

-249-

My ball was resting on a tree stump.

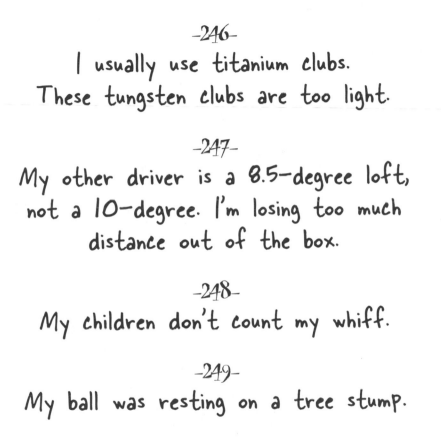

69

-250-

I'm getting married
in three hours—
it's hard to
concentrate.

70

The lessons I took on the Internet are not working the way they said they would.

My ball was wedged in the corner between the grass and sand.
I had no shot.

My country club's fairways are much better. These conditions are unplayable.

It's too humid.
My shirt is sticking to my body.

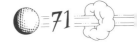

-255-

My allergies are killing me.
I can't deal with all the pressure.

-256-

My regular caddie was arrested.
This guy is an idiot—he doesn't know a
3-wood from a 5-wood.

-257-

The lie I had wasn't perfectly perfect.

-258-

I broke my pitching wedge
the last time I played.
This sand wedge has too much loft.

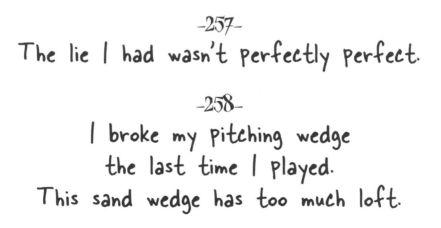

-259-

I had the club face opened
too much in the bunker.

-260-

The greens are too fast.
They are like ice.

-261-

I can't play with these golf balls.
The numbers are too high.

-262-

I thought if the ball is above
your feet it will slice.

-263-

My athlete's foot is causing me to miss-hit.

-264-

The chipping area was closed at 3:00 A.M. (that's when I came to practice).

-265-

I just moved to a new house and my back is aching. I have no follow-through.

-266-

I play better with a hard golf ball. These soft ones are for the pros.

–267–

My clubs are too old.
These wooden shafts don't have the right flex.

–268–

I keep moving my putter
when I swing my shoulders.

–269–

The greens I normally play on are much slower.

–270–

The marshal told me to lay up on this hole.
I am a fool for listening.

-271-

The ball was wedged up against the tree.
I had no shot.

-272-

The grass bunker gave me no shot.
Who the hell designed this course?

-273-

The carpet in my living room
doesn't break like this green.

-274-

This copper bracelet is too tight on my wrist.
I can't hold on to the club.

275

I keep second-guessing my shots.

-276-

Your cigar smoke keeps getting
in my eyes when I putt.

-277-

The clubs I ordered on the
Internet haven't arrived yet.
I'm stuck with these old ones.

-278-

There is too much goose crap on the course.

-279-

To hell with the tournament.
I don't look good in a green jacket anyway.

-280-
I never got comfortable over the ball.

-281-
I don't like this gripless putter,
but my broker gave it to me.

-282-
I'm taking my club back too fast.

-283-
The guy on The Golf Channel hit
these clubs perfectly every time.
They don't seem to work for me.

-284-

My wife didn't wash my lucky golf shirt.

-285-

I thought when I turned 40
I could play from the gold tees.

-286-

I can't judge the distance of my ball
in this cool December air.

-287-

My dog was sick last night.
I didn't get any sleep.

-288-

My ball ricocheted off that water pump and went into the woods. Shouldn't I get a do-over?

-289-

My shirt is itchy. I bet you my wife forgot to use the fabric softener again.

-290-

Titanium balls fly too far for my ability.

-291-

From 300 yards out it looks like the green slopes away. I should have laid up.

81

-292-

The guys behind us are pushing us.
They are making me nervous.

-293-

The snow keeps getting in my eyes.

-294-

My pants are too tight—
but I think the beer girl likes them.

-295-

There is no way this is a
500-yard hole—it's only 490.

-296-

I had a root canal last month.
It still hurts when I golf.

-297-

I got whiplash when you started the cart.
Now my neck hurts.

-298-

I had to take a drop.
The speed limit sign was in the way.

-299-

I can't play well unless I'm clean-shaven.

-301-
That putt should have gone in.
My ball must be lopsided.

-302-
This green isn't fair.
It's surrounded by bunkers.

-303-
The rye grass isn't fair.
I can't play on anything but bluegrass.

-304-
Did you see that? The head of my
driver flew off during my swing!

-305-

I lost my contact lens on the last hole.
I'm playing one-eyed.

-306-

I haven't refilled my medication this week.

-307-

My ball must have hit a sprinkler head.
It ended up in the water.
I never go in the water.

-308-

I only play well when I bet.

-309-

I must need new glasses.
I can't seem to read a putt today.

-310-

I hate playing on Sundays.
They won't serve me beer until 11:00 A.M.

-311-

That putt was short because
I'm using those South American golf balls.
It was a whole revolution short.

-312-

I pulled the putt because an
ant crawled on my shoe.

–313–

That car door slammed while I was swinging!

–314–

I didn't have a 3–wood so
I had to use my 5–wood.

–315–

These are my wife's golf shoes.
Mine are being respiked.

–316–

I lost the ball in the fog, but it was
headed straight for the green.
Someone must have picked it up.

-317-
You were moving when I was attempting my birdie putt.

-318-
When you leaned on your putter, it left an indentation on the green.

-319-
If the lip on the hole weren't pushed up, it would have fallen in.

-320-
I would rather be home cleaning the basement than playing on this cow pasture they call a golf course.

-321-

My hands are sweaty and the
clubhouse had no soap.

-322-

A bunch of hackers must have torn up
the green. I can't play competitively
under these circumstances.

-323-

My subscription to Golf Digest
ran out this month.

-324-

I was better before I retired.
I just don't have time to golf anymore.

-325-

I drank too much coffee—I have the shakes.

-326-
The cable went out at home last night, and I missed my final lesson on The Golf Channel.

-327-
The ball doesn't fly as far here as in Canada.

-328-
My lucky hat is in my wife's car. Otherwise that putt would have dropped.

-329-
I don't like these balls I bought over the Internet. They fly too far.

–330–

The bookstore was out of Golf Magazine.

–331–

My hat is too tight;
it's giving me a headache.

–332–

I'm in the middle of a divorce.

–333–

I have a hard time when
I'm playing with you guys.
It's hard playing with your best friends.

The airline ground crew cracked my driver.
Now I have to tee off with my 3-wood.

This new ball I'm playing has much
less spin than my old one.
I thought that shot would check up.

The GPS on this cart is way off.

That car dealership overcharged me so
I can't afford the good balls.

-338-

I can't tee off unless a
crowd of people is watching.

-339-

The alarm on my watch
went off during my backswing.

-340-

I only par holes that I like.

-341-

The dew on the green slowed up my putt.

-342-

I forgot to take my vitamins this morning.
Now I'm out of energy.

-343-

Your cell phone should have been turned off.

-344-

I need yellow lenses for my sunglasses.
I'm getting too many ultraviolet rays.

-345-

I thought this little shark on my shirt
would make me play better.

-346-

I'm exhausted—the batteries in my
TV remote died yesterday.

-347-

My thumb wasn't aligned with the club's axis.

-348-

I never looked at the whole green.
It slopes left.

-349-

The shade of that tree threw off my
depth perception.

-350-

My usual group is much better than you guys. They raise my level of play.

98

–351–

I can't play unless I have sex prior to playing.

–352–

I have sarcoidosis; I haven't been able to play.

–353–

One of my shoelaces broke on the backswing.

–354–

I haven't been able to play
since the auto accident.
Too bad I can't sue for strokes.

–355–

I can't focus on golf when my
football team is playing.

–356–

I'm too concerned about how my wife is
playing to worry about my own game.

–357–

I just can't envision the shot—and
that's the key to the whole game.

–358–

Your golf shirt is too bright.
Who the hell dresses you?

-359-

I never flared my left foot.

-360-

The club only had small buckets
available at the range.
I needed a large one.

-361-

I teed the ball too low.

-362-

I can't concentrate since I got fired.

-363-

I've been preoccupied with the budget debate going on in Congress.

-364-

It's much windier on the West Coast. I need at least 30 knots to play properly.

-365-

The sun dried out the green. The balls are rolling too fast.

-366-

Polo is my strong game.

-367-

I can only make the 10-footers; the 3-footers throw me off.

-368-

I should have focused on the spot behind the ball.

-369-

I was in Seattle the last three weeks and all it did was rain. I couldn't practice.

-370-

Since filing for bankruptcy, I can only golf twice a week.

-371-

I thought the blue markers meant 100 yards.

-372-

This Alzheimer's makes me
forget where my ball landed.

-373-

I only started playing again last month.

-374-

I can't golf regularly for religious reasons.

-375-

I thought cross-handed putting was supposed to be the answer.

-376-
I thought the white stake on the side is what I was aiming for. I didn't realize it was out of bounds.

-377-
My body is swaying too much from the alcohol.

-378-
I swung down too steeply on the ball.

-379-
My feet must not have been parallel to the target.

-380-

I moved my right knee on the backswing,
creating an illusion of power
which was improperly assessed.

-381-

Since shooting 68,
I haven't been able to break 100.

-382-

I can't afford golf lessons.

-383-

My body tipped forward on the backswing,
which opened the face of
the 3-wood, creating a slice.

-384-
I was bent too far forward over the ball to get spin on it.

-385-
The wind held the ball up in the air. I knew I should have gone to services this morning.

-386-
I feel guilty using tees made in China.

-387-
My ball landed in a fairway divot because some lazy-butt didn't replace his.

-388-

The greenskeeper aerated the fairways
too early in the season.
I can't get any roll on the ball.

-389-

I had a clump of mud on my ball,
causing it to go hard to the left.

-390-

The golf instruction videotape I bought
didn't teach me how to putt.

-391-

The driving range wouldn't let me
use any of my woods, only irons.

–392–

My putter shaft must be bent slightly.

–393–

The water in the creek wasn't
this high last week.
That would have been a great shot.

–394–

I had my knees bent too far and
I got way under the ball.

–395–

I'm getting old. I used to beat you
all the time when you were kids.

-396-

The only tree on the entire
hole and I've hit it twice.

-397-

My ball has a scuff on it from
hitting the pin on the last par-3.
Now it spins too much around its axis.

-398-

I haven't had time to practice my putting.

-399-

I never noticed this trap before.
I usually hit the green from 275 out.

111

-400-

I've only been golfing
for a couple of years—
I don't have my
swing down yet.

112

-401-
This putter stinks.
It has no lines on it to set up the putt.

-402-
I need a beer and the cart
girl hasn't been around.

-403-
My short game is my strong suit, not driving.

-404-
On impact, my hips went through too early
and it opened up my swing, causing
the ball to angle improperly.

-405-

I put way too much spin on the ball and it rolled off the green, down the hill, bounced off that rake and fell into the trap.

-406-

I usually play with the club pro, but he isn't here to give me tips.

-407-

The wind blew sand in my eyes.

-408-

I took too much of a divot and the ball came up short.

-409-

I pulled my club too far back on the backswing, creating insufficient torque on the forward transition.

-410-

The beer cart girl went home. I can't relax.

-411-

I only play well with forged clubs; cast clubs are too soft.

-412-

I have a difficult time accepting a bad bounce after hitting a great shot.

-413-
I only read three angles to the putt.
I should have taken all four.
I'm too lazy.

-414-
I just choked...again.

-415-
The ball just broke too much to the left.

-416-
That leaf blew in front of my putt!

-417-

I rotated my hands too far to the left, which made the club face open at an improper point of the swing.

-418-

The guy on the other green yelled right when I was in my backswing.

-419-

I aimed my shoulder too far left of the target.

-420-

I was standing too close to the ball.

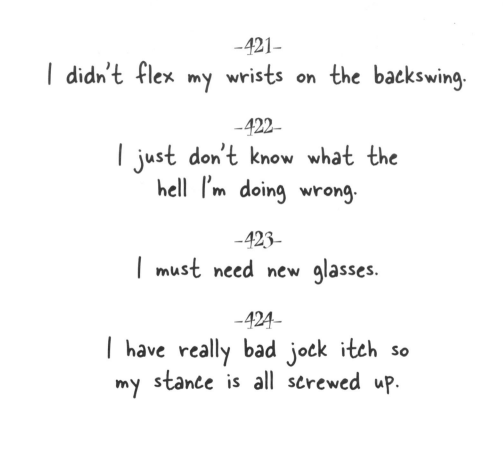

–421–

I didn't flex my wrists on the backswing.

–422–

I just don't know what the
hell I'm doing wrong.

–423–

I must need new glasses.

–424–

I have really bad jock itch so
my stance is all screwed up.

-425-

My hair gel evaporated and now my hair keeps getting in my eyes.

-426-

I was kicked off of my high school golf team.
I haven't played since.
It's too emotionally painful.

-427-

I just don't play well in the sun, rain, clouds,
snow, or sleet—I lose my focus.

-428-

The golf seminar I wanted
to go to was sold out.

-429-

I can't get my mental checklist
in its proper order.

-430-
My dog ran away this morning,
so I didn't have time to warm up.

-431-
It's so humid, I came out of the trap on
the last hole and the wind blew the sand in
my face and now it's stuck and I can't see.

-432-
My calves hurt from running.

-433-
I can only get enthusiastic about sex.
Golf just doesn't do it, so I don't try.

-434-
After that last shot, I'm just
too embarrassed to try.

-435-
My brother took my good golf glove.

-436-
I have two teenage daughters,
both of whom are going out tonight.
Need I say more?

-437-
The leaky faucet at home kept me up all night.

-438-
I just can't get that triple bogey
out of my head.

-439-
I get so excited when I play that I can't relax.
I love this game!

-440-
I am only out here to avoid
my mother-in-law.

-441-
My calculator must have run out of batteries.
Put me down for a three.

-442-
I am constantly overestimating my ability.

-443-
I am committed to my wife.
Golf has always come second.

-444-
I only care if I look good, not how I golf.

-445-
I only took up the game
to get away from the house.
I don't really care if I'm good.

-446-

I only play for the camaraderie.

-447-

I am so excited about the World Series
game tonight, I can't focus.

-448-

I knew I should have bought
those rain gloves last week.

-449-

My lucky argyles are in my other golf bag.
I can't putt without them.

125

-451-

I can never get my last shot off my mind.

-452-

My ex-girlfriend's brother-in-law is
an old golf pro. He used to give me free
golf lessons. If we had stayed together,
I could have made that putt.

-453-

I only play for personal, non-substantive goals.

-454-

Golf isn't fun if it's competitive,
so I don't try hard.

-455-
The warden wouldn't let me practice
all those years in prison.

-456-
I usually play the slice.
Now I'm hitting it straight.
I just don't understand this game.

-457-
I never even saw that tree next to
the pond next to the forest.

-458-
I thought the red stakes were a
target towards the green.

-459-

My cat chewed up my Thursday
golf underwear.
I had to wear Sunday's.

-460-

I'm not used to betting more
than a quarter a hole.

-461-

Some idiot ahead of us keeps leaving
sunflower seeds on the green.

-462-

I thought this was a par—6.
I was just laying up.

-463-

I have the yips; I just don't know what to do.

-464-

The big mistake I always make is
expecting to play better than I do.
I have trouble handling disappointment.

-465-

My mom used to iron all my socks.
I just can't get the crease the right way.

-466-

I don't care how I score when I'm young.
My only goal is to live long enough
to shoot lower than my age.

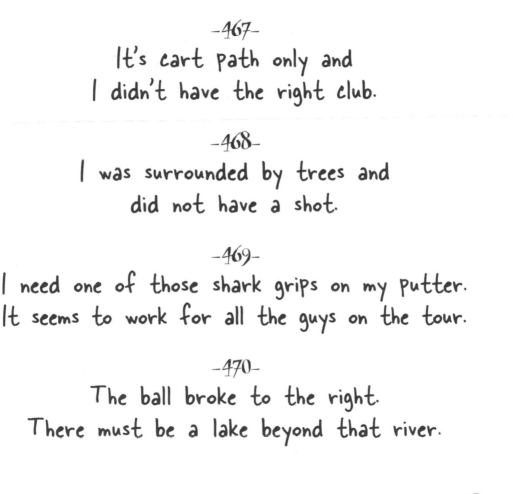

-467-

It's cart path only and
I didn't have the right club.

-468-

I was surrounded by trees and
did not have a shot.

-469-

I need one of those shark grips on my putter.
It seems to work for all the guys on the tour.

-470-

The ball broke to the right.
There must be a lake beyond that river.

-471-

I thought you aim halfway
when chipping with a 7-iron.

-472-

I dropped my left shoulder and hooked the ball.

-473-

Bermuda grass sucks
My club keeps getting stuck.

-474-

I can only chip with an 8-iron.
I must have left it on the last hole—or
maybe you are trying to sabotage my round.

—475—

I play for the exercise, not the score.

-476-

I shot a 71 on this course last time.
Then again, it was on my computer.

-477-

I played too much softball last week;
I'm hitting the ball too flat.

-478-

The tee box has no grass in it.
I only play well at well-manicured courses.

-479-

My tempo is off since the
incident with the ball washer.

-480-
I usually hit the driver off the fairway fine. The greenskeeper must be doing a poor job.

-481-
I can only get motivated to play golf after watching Caddyshack.

-482-
I'm used to playing in Alaska. When I hit the pond, it's usually frozen. This isn't fair.

-483-
I need to change my putting technique.

-484-

It was easier to putt when I wasn't good.
Now it's just too much pressure.

-485-

My golf bag is too small.
I usually have a larger selection of clubs.

-486-

These sneakers just don't give me the proper
support required for my ankles.

-487-

I'm used to playing courses with pine trees.
The oaks are distracting.

-488-

I putted really well on the
miniature golf course last night.

-489-

I hit that well. The golf gods
must be against me today.

-490-

I should have used the putter
to get out of the bunker.

-491-

That duct tape just doesn't
work as well as real grips.

-492-

Golf is about etiquette, not about playing well.

-493-

I picked up my foot on my backswing.

-494-

I'm only playing for the charity.

-495-

What do you mean, winter rules
aren't allowed in the summer?

-496-

I didn't come to play golf.
I wanted to see the Cubs in spring training.

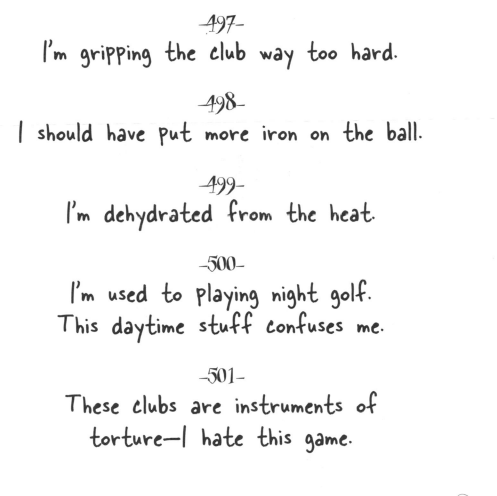

-497-

I'm gripping the club way too hard.

-498-

I should have put more iron on the ball.

-499-

I'm dehydrated from the heat.

-500-

I'm used to playing night golf.
This daytime stuff confuses me.

-501-

These clubs are instruments of
torture—I hate this game.

About the Author

Justin J. Exner is an airline executive with a BA in Aviation Business from Embry-Riddle Aeronautical University in Daytona Beach, Florida, and an MBA from Franklin University in Columbus, Ohio. He has played golf all over the world, and never makes a bad golf shot without a good reason. Justin golfs regularly and three-putts very frequently. He lives with his family in Haymarket, Virginia.